Shaban Mohammadi
Mahmoud Lari Dashtbayaz
Ali Mohammadi

Application of Computer Science in Accounting and Audit

Shaban Mohammadi
Mahmoud Lari Dashtbayaz
Ali Mohammadi

Application of Computer Science in Accounting and Audit

Basics, Concepts, Methods

LAP LAMBERT Academic Publishing

Impressum / Imprint

Bibliografische Information der Deutschen Nationalbibliothek: Die Deutsche Nationalbibliothek verzeichnet diese Publikation in der Deutschen Nationalbibliografie; detaillierte bibliografische Daten sind im Internet über http://dnb.d-nb.de abrufbar.
Alle in diesem Buch genannten Marken und Produktnamen unterliegen warenzeichen-, marken- oder patentrechtlichem Schutz bzw. sind Warenzeichen oder eingetragene Warenzeichen der jeweiligen Inhaber. Die Wiedergabe von Marken, Produktnamen, Gebrauchsnamen, Handelsnamen, Warenbezeichnungen u.s.w. in diesem Werk berechtigt auch ohne besondere Kennzeichnung nicht zu der Annahme, dass solche Namen im Sinne der Warenzeichen- und Markenschutzgesetzgebung als frei zu betrachten wären und daher von jedermann benutzt werden dürften.

Bibliographic information published by the Deutsche Nationalbibliothek: The Deutsche Nationalbibliothek lists this publication in the Deutsche Nationalbibliografie; detailed bibliographic data are available in the Internet at http://dnb.d-nb.de.
Any brand names and product names mentioned in this book are subject to trademark, brand or patent protection and are trademarks or registered trademarks of their respective holders. The use of brand names, product names, common names, trade names, product descriptions etc. even without a particular marking in this work is in no way to be construed to mean that such names may be regarded as unrestricted in respect of trademark and brand protection legislation and could thus be used by anyone.

Coverbild / Cover image: www.ingimage.com

Verlag / Publisher:
LAP LAMBERT Academic Publishing
ist ein Imprint der / is a trademark of
OmniScriptum GmbH & Co. KG
Heinrich-Böcking-Str. 6-8, 66121 Saarbrücken, Deutschland / Germany
Email: info@lap-publishing.com

Herstellung: siehe letzte Seite /
Printed at: see last page
ISBN: 978-3-659-69952-8

Application of Computer Science in Accounting and Audit

Table of Contents

4

Chapter I

Concept System Accounting and Information Systems

Defined in the humanities, the system can be set from the elements missions or achieve a specific purpose designed and built with quality and quantity determined by the quantity and quality of the data are combined to define. 1. collection system the elements that come together to achieve a common goal and clear, so that there is an interaction between the elements of a relationship. the next feature of the system, there is order in the relations between elements in the sense that every element of a role. accounting an information system by which information about the financial activities of identification, registration, the classification is summarized in order to enable informed decision making Is available to all users. accounting information system, a system through which information and statements. collected and arranged the financing and the use made of it. the system performance accounting information quality of information provided to it and the proper management of its operation It depends. any weakness and lack of efficiency and security of information systems, accounting, reduction efficiency, productivity and numerous problems in the planning and decision-making will found. Since the accounting information system to recognize and understand how the system functions accounting includes methods of collecting data related to financial activities and events and how to convert data into information that can manage them in the organization used and how to ensure the accessibility and reliance on the information, emphasizes a an organization is vital and basic systems. the auditors today an important role in ensuring the users Information is performed. auditors should be reviewed to ensure the maintenance of security systems. accounting information. auditors are aware that without the security of information systems. accounting, managers will be able to provide reliable, accurate information. it may be financial reports due to the lack of security in the accounting systems of distortion and manipulation be. however, internal auditors can provide security in information systems accountants have an important role, since they are directly responsible for helping to manage companies to improve efficiency and effectiveness are responsible.

Accounting Information Systems Security

Security is one of the most important technological issues and the importance of it is due to in adequate security in a system of any reliability in reporting the information required to Persons within or outside the organization, as well as the opportunity to prevent counterfeiting, tampering and fraud increases. importance and reliance of financial information for today's decision is a clear public interest groups in the world

6

today can safely be he said that any decision of the administrative and financial results is sought, therefore, to manage any the decision to reliable financial information is required. expertise in information systems and technology support they lead to the qualification for the accounting profession. but, unfortunately, training the main body includes business information systems security is not designed to accommodate it the following are proposed. Providing conditions for specifying the location of information systems security as part of an accounting education; Providing a number of scientific and practical guide for teachers of Information systems accounting information systems have a tendency to develop and supply security.

Security breaches in accounting information systems

There are many internal and external factors that cause the system security flaws. With the Most important reason is related to the organization of those assets and Accounting systems of access. Internal organizational problems such controls internal weak, weak policies and lack of integrity in high levels of staff The main reasons of security threats. Employees may be done for many reasons Computer Crime And try to steal from work. The most common reasons could be revenge, revenge, debt And lack of internal controls is personal. Today the business is very competitive and push employees And increased stress as a result, they may feel that they can be worked over Asked for and received less pay than usual. However, if the same issues Serious personal difficulties faced on the job are also increasing their motivation for fraud Will, by the terms of this equation if the weak internal controls and available technology Notebook computers will be added that will help the offense. The opportunity to make a real and objective aspects of fraud cases.

Goals in Information Systems Security

Completeness of information: the information is reliable, comprehensive, complete and sound Therefore information should not be manipulated by unauthorized persons. Confidential information to unauthorized individuals or legal persons should inform themselves in Are available. Acceptable Use of Information: Each user is allowed to the extent that the information is allowed Received and is available for special applications. Availability of information: Information must be timely and quickly provide authorized users Place. authorized user when information needs to be able to access it.

Security threats in accounting information systems

Security threats based on the source of the problem and its cause and intent of Committed respondents are divided into three categories. 1. thdydat internal vs. external threats by source Starters.the staff are the most important source of internal security threats while hackers, Disasters and natural events as a major source of external threats to consider. Some Believe that internal staff to potentially dangerous enemies of the system And in most cases, errors or unauthorized access to information is the main root of the problem The security of the system. 2.thdydat human versus non-human threats by creating Manufacturer. Human security threats are threats that originate from human actions and can Are accidental and inadvertent or deliberate. Human errors can Safety and security threats in accounting information systems Format errors caused by negligence or neglect or crimes occur. Type I error occurs when That the person doing the correct handicapped and Type II error occurs when That's going to do what is wrong, or it is prohibited from Other inhumane threats generally technical threats such as system or hardware malfunction or Related systems or software problems caused by natural disasters such as flood and earthquake. Some technical threats may be associated with human actions, such as entering a Virus to infect the system via software. 3. Random unintentional threats against malicious threats on the plan And intent of the perpetrator subject Unintentional threats are threats of vindictive and malicious intent originated

Not. While the threat of deliberate threats that have malicious intent, such as Sabotage, computer fraud and misuse of authorized access to their systems. Wrongful acts that although the costs imposed on the organization Are modifiable and can be prevented from occurring through training and supervision. But actions Generally lead to cybercrime involving intentional destruction of system components, removing or changing Records and files .... and to eliminate the production of information or misinformation, are. (Lakh et al. 1992) on the question of security in information systems based on a model Four subsequent to the conclusion that it is possible security threats, such as the threat of acts of Employees or failure of internal or external, such as natural disasters or acts of hackers Are. According to this model, the agent is no longer any threat, some threats Human actions are the result of natural events or human while others are Finally, apply regardless of the source can be intentional or unintentional. In studies conducted concluded that accountants should Be aware of threats to information security, such as the technology rapidly Is changing as well as information security risks, and these risks are changing rapidly

8

One of the major concerns of each economic unit. The establishment of an appropriate system of internal controls and procedures include good employment and training programs suitable for the occurrence of cybercrime The stand has losses to a minimum. (Daly and Hmkaran2000) in their investigation concluded that measurement of security Accounting information systems and developing new fashion to the first key Be taken into account and the ability to measure the awareness of security and stability of the regulatory system Depends on the core components of information security, including password, hide data, participation Employees and the protection against computer viruses. (Weiss, 2001) in relation to computer information systems concluded that Technology advancements have enabled companies to a computer to transfer the activities They were previously performed manually. (Ji et al. 2005) in their research Concluded that the problems related to information systems have a number of companies to Disclosure is important weaknesses. Risks in the system The information comes from various sources that, if ignored, can be related And the reliance of financial information to destroy and lead to incorrect decisions by stakeholders Be different. Using the system New risks associated. Managers should seek to identify potential risks arising from Threats of internal control in computer-based accounting information systems and Using a variety of models to assess the effects of these hazards. Most operations office in the organization Today on the accounting information system and on the other hand, given that Safety and security threats in accounting information systems Chains of cause), Globalization, unauthorized access, etc. (The system threatens the Security should be one of the most important issues on the agenda of every company. Risk can be examined from quantitative analysis, Qualitative analysis of the computer and check that the further analysis of large organizations And medium enterprises, but in small organizations, adequate funding and staff To perform this analysis, but there is a minimum security assessment must be done. About the relationship between internal audit and security Internal audit and information security should be part of a group Employees work together because information security tools and methods of operation And technological resources to protect their organization's internal audit Periodic feedback on the types of activities that contribute to improving the security of information provided. Accounting information systems as a basis for management decision making when managers are able The decisions that the information provided in addition to the features of the system And timeliness, security is embedded in the ability to use information Guarantee. Nowadays you can find an organization that does not use the computer networks and Valuable information is not stored. all these organizations and low-speed connections Speed internet. On the other hand, is equipped with high penetration power tools and cheap The price of the software and hardware in order to benefit the economy, satisfy curiosity and disturbing These networks. the establishment of an effective and dynamic security policy, the duty of every organization Data Protection and its reputation. Part of the task of managing information security management information security objectives, Examine the barriers to achieving these goals and is responsible for providing the necessary solutions. The task of implementing security management and control of the security system's performance And finally, to try to keep the system always up to date, so managers and Accountants should be familiar with the types of threats and methods of security in information systems to Managed to secure their information systems. The threat can not be completely Specific measures may be ruined, but it is somewhat limited. Security Accepted accounting information systems increases the reliability and trustworthiness Financial reports, which leads to the usefulness of the information contained in financial reports The decision to use inside and outside the organization.

Viruses, types and potential destruction

It is difficult to detect attacks by viruses. The nature of virus attacks in several Years ago has changed. In the past, such attacks by hackers intent to sabotage But now most of the attacks were carried out with the aim of financial abuse There. For example, when you download music, you're going to be targeted by hackers Stay as long as you are listening to this music, you may be viruses Multiply your system and steal your information Rvd.bh example, Latest Flame Virus by the West against Iran's security systems are designed, Unlike Stuxnet, which is designed just for spying and collecting data, the Virus from computer monitor to turn on a computer microphone, taking photos The recorded conversations. The information gathered on the source of the virus is transmitted publisher A. A computer virus, is a computer program that can replicate itself And infect the computer. Word wrong about some malware virus, promotional tools Which is also referred annoying proliferation. A computer virus to the original form or with Create your changes, from one computer to another over the Internet, USB or Disc moving parts. Their chances of spreading to other viruses can Computers by infecting files on a system or network increases. Viruses are similar to all the other system resources such as memory and disk space Hardware, CPU and other resources will be able to carry out dangerous actions Them. For example, to delete the files on the physical disc and supports provided by the system Accounting information is destroyed or the entire hard drive with all the deleted data. Common types of viruses can be divided into the following categories: Boot sector, which began at the start of the operating system is active. Macro: The macro programming languages such as Word and Excel uses. Viruses executable files: When you run existing applications, including systems Accounting information in the computer starts to operate. Polymorphic viruses, the virus-infected files as they appear. The That uses encryption algorithms and also cleans traces of your own, Detection and diagnosis of these viruses is difficult. Hidden viruses: These viruses are trying to counter the operating system and software Viruses are hidden. Other program interferes with the security, Trojan horses, worms, logic bombs, and the Grouped together, these programs are very dangerous and can lead to serious damage Into the computer.

Security policies and proposed methods to prevent the risks of viruses

Large and small organizations need to create security policies about the use of Computers and computer networks are secure. Security policies, set Rules for the use of computers and computer networks in which all tasks Members are precisely specified and, if necessary, warnings to users about the use of Resources available in the network. Knowledge of all users who have access to all or part of the network There should be regular with respect to the formulation of policies, during the training Due to the continuous and targeted policies edited. Some of these policies and ways Prevent the risk of viruses as follows: Cyber responsibility as a citizen: If you use the Internet Bug Tracker, you as a member of the international community or the cyber citizen, and as such An ordinary citizen has certain responsibilities that must be open to them. Use anti-virus software, a computer virus is a program that Can infiltrate your computer and cause great damage. anti Software To protect against computer viruses and known viruses, Are designed. Given that the daily supply of new viruses transpires, Anti-virus programs must be updated regularly and frequently. To get Complete and efficient service from the manufacturers of anti-virus never Do not use unauthorized reproduction of viruses. No activation e-mail sent by unknown sources and Anonymous: e-mail sent by unknown sources should always be removed. The files that are sent as attachments with an e-mail notice Thus, even if this type of e-mails from friends and acquaintances (The. Some receive your .exe files responsibility), especially if you have a connection Responsible for distributing viruses and can cause numerous problems such as permanently Their files. Passwords that are difficult to detect them, and use them Keep confidential. Many computer users care about Keep your password and this can cause enormous problems to them, The. Passwords that are easy to recognize or guess the appropriate options Not related. At specified intervals and continually attempted to change your password here. Never give your password to any other parties. To choose a password Through a combination of numbers, letters and symbols used to estimate and track them by Illegal, is difficult. Use a firewall to protect computers: Installation and configuration A firewall should not be difficult. a firewall, access control system It denied attackers and prevent the theft of information on Computer performs. regularly backing up valuable data on your computer in Intervals on the basis of a specific program of valuable information on Computer and information systems, accounting and financial data backed up on them Storage media such as CDs store. Download and install updated regularly for flaws, flaws in Regularly in operating systems and applications are discovered. companies Manufacturer software including accounting information systems, to act quickly to provide Updated versions of the updates that users must send their name and on Install on your system. In this respect it is important to regularly sites the producers of the software has been made to provide an update on the case, it download and install the system. Computer viruses, threats to security ... Periodic review and evaluation of computer security, computer security situation in The time period studied, and if you can do it Your use of relevant experts. Turn the Internet connection when not using the Internet as a road Two-way. You can send or receive information above. Turn the relationship with Internet in cases where it is not needed, allowing others access to your computer disclaimer Well. Not sharing resources available on computer users that their identity Unknown Operating System installed on a computer, it may be possible to Sharing of resources such as files with other network users, to provide. This feature can be enabled on a specific security threat. So then Need to disable the feature, the action is applied. Proper use of Memory Stick: Memory Stick, one of the main routes The virus is transmitted, the use of which should be noted. Use the services of experts in the field of security experts Out. The successful management of an enterprise, regardless of the fundamental role of information act That's impossible. Financial information is a valuable business asset. Run As a mechanism of protection of information security, an integral component in the successful management of the organization. Nowadays, computer viruses are one of the main causes damage to the area of security. In this The theft of financial information is a major objective of viruses. Lack of attention to the potential risks Viruses and lack of proactive on this issue, it may be irreversible problems Create it. another aspect that should be considered, subject to audit. Part of Auditors should check the reliability of accounting information systems security. Auditors are aware that without the security of information systems, accounting, managers are able to Information provided will be accurate and reliable. This makes it doubly important security issue A. The proposals, which should be expressed as a user, the laws governing the Internet We observe, for preventing contamination of anti-virus computer use; We will remove anonymous emails, passwords are used for determining the level of access We do not have access to a good firewall design invaders, the temporal Backup data we update our information systems, the security Computer to periodically check in when you do not need internet connection to its We cut to the Internet, accessible from the files in the computer and accounting information systems Anonymous maintain, as appropriate, use the Memory Stick Finally, the Comments security experts also take advantage.

Chapter II

Cluster computing

Computing cluster in a cluster computer, a group of free computers that work together and in many ways PC can be viewed as a complex behavior. components of the cluster computers usually are connected to each other through the network. clusters usually speed, create redundancy to increase accessibility continuous and secure the position of the error configured.

Grid computing

Grid computing is further confused by cloud computing; two things are quite different. grid computing, several sources' computers in a network to work concurrently on uses on an issue. This is mostly used. when will be considered a scientific or technical problem. Famous examples Is. Home the search for an extraterrestrial intelligence project the project will allow people around the world until the unemployment, the search for signs of intelligent computer extraterrestrial be used.

Cloud computing

The persian to the cloud, (cloud computing) term cloud computing and cloud computing have been translated, structural make it look like a cloud mass that users can to access applications from any-where in the world are. So, the next cloud computing instead of the term cloud computing will be used, can help network, as (virtuale machines) virtual machines a new method for creating dynamic new generation of data centers considered. thus, in the world of computing is rapidly software development is going to run it on Individual PCs, as a service to millions consumers are. as mentioned above most of the time was wrong grid computing to cloud computing will. to prevent the error from the comparison of the two offers.

Comparison of cloud computing and lace

The major difference is that the computing cloud computing and computing net screen. a huge project is divided among multiple computers, the resources it employs. the growing popularity of cloud computing is that it represents a variety of technologies are being used more and more for Popularity as one of the new Internet technologies like any computer innovations quickly to the business world accounting also opens the way. Therefore, this paper attempts to address this issue and the impact of cloud computing technology on the accounting profession check. The paper is organized as follows: In section 2, the cloud, the Section 3 reviews the accounting profession cloud computing technology, the section 4. Finally, section 5 is to evaluate

and compare models and technologies conclusions and suggestions for future work
are presented.

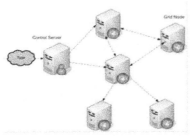

But cloud computing has allowed several small computer program Can be run
simultaneously on multiple computers.

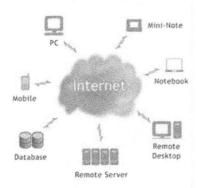

Figure 2: View of cloud computing .

Computing net can only be used for applications who have the ability to run in
parallel, but in computing There is not a cloud in the corresponding fields. In a
concluding generally it can be said that the ultimate goal of cloud computing services
provide the highest End users are. the purpose computing net calculation heavy and
above the net.

The acceptance of a variety of computing

The popularity of the mentioned three different types of calculations, the google's
search engine visibility is evaluated the result is shown in Figure 3. this study shows
that cluster computing is now more than two other less popular, computing the
second screen Is, and cloud computing are far from being Increase people's attention
more.

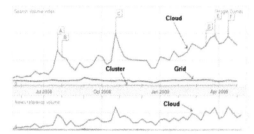

Figure 3: Check the Google cluster system acceptance, net and a cloud in the years 2008 , 2009.

The growing popularity of cloud computing is that it represents avariety of technologies are being used more and more for Popularity as one of the new Internet technologies like any computer innovations quickly to the business world accounting also opens the way. therefore, this paper attempts to address this issue and the impact of cloud computing technology on the accounting profession check. the paper is organized as follows: In section 2, the cloud, the Section 3 reviews the accounting profession cloud computing technology, the section 4. finally, section 5 is to evaluate and compare models and technologies conclusions and suggestions for future work are presented. What is cloud computing? With the development of computer equipment and dependence Most of us in the digital world, companies have to are seeking to accelerate the promotion of their services to customers. Naturally, any company that is faster and better services Its users will be the winner of this field. In this Cloud the issue by large companies and looking extremely small and huge investments have started on it. Indeed, what is cloud computing its definition. before the definition of cloud computing, the better the meaning of the word "cloud" be clarified. The cloud is a metaphorical term that refers to the Internet [6]. and a system which may ultimately distributed and parallel computers connected through a series of virtual and physical form different levels of service to one or more computing resource ally based on agreements between service provider and consumer provides services provided [16]. In general it can be said that cloud abstract image of a network and the great bulk of it is unknown, it is not clear how consists of processing resources. Every dimension of time and space components are not known, as well as hardware and software instead this software is not apparent mass. But the definition of cloud computing is to say that, since it now It has been accepted for presentation, however, most experts on the part of the definition of this phenomenon is vote. and who defines cloud computing Wikipedia : "cloud computing is a computing model

17

based on large computer networks Internet is the new model for the supply, delivery and consumption IT services (including hardware, software, data, and other shared computing resources) by using the Internet that "[4]. cloud computing to provide information technology solutions to manner similar to utilities (water, telephone, electricity, etc.) suggests. Just like electricity, water and gas. you have the Equipment and electricity, gas and water use at home or work you do not need a generator of electricity, gas and water system at home you, but for a certain fee, you rent it. now if you use more or less, the cost of consumption you will pay for itself, without the hardware components be aware of the services and infrastructure [10.16]. America cloud NIST «National Institute of Standards and Technology» It is also defined as: "Cloud computing is a model for an easy access on user demand through the network to a set of processing resources are subject to change and configuration (eg, networks, servers, space Storage, applications, and services) that can be accessed with minimal labor or intervention providers Service provided or to be released soon. " The cloud model, and improves the availability of five the important characteristics, three service models, and four deployment models .

Characteristics of Cloud

Computing features include a choice of cloud-based service request, broad network access, resource integration, flexibility, speed, agility, scalability, high reliability and service-oriented Is.

Models of Service Cloud service models or types of services

in Indeed, in this kind of technology on the Internet Be made available to the users. all cloud services can Be classified according to these sources, and usually refers to "the as a service "and used words are given. based on ANSI NIST cloud computing services offered in 3 forms SaaS, (Software as a Service), IaaS (Infrastructure as a Service), Paas (Platform as a Service) [14].

Software as a Service (SaaS)

Cloud services, applications or software as a service, Software as a service over the Internet, and thus the need to install software on the client computer and to make it easier to maintain and support. Because the customer cloud infrastructure, network, servers, operating systems, space manage or control the underlying storage or application does not. this is primarily a software application commercial known .

Cloud platform as a service (PaaS)

Cloud platform services, computing platform (often on infrastructure Implemented cloud and cloud applications feeds) into if the service. in this model, instead of software, platform (platform) as a service. the platform as a service, the software can be used without the cost and complexity of buying and management of hardware and software (such as Java, Python, .NET, Etc.) and provide web hosting services expanded Software developers to create new applications or previous development programs need to be developed spending.

Cloud Infrastructure as a Service (IaaS)

Cloud infrastructure services or infrastructure as a service, Computer infrastructure (typically a physical or virtual platform a) to provide the service. users instead of buying Hardware, software, data center space or network equipment, all this infrastructure as a fully outsourced service buy. usually based billing services (out-sourcing) The utility computing model (water, telephone, electricity, etc.), the amount of resources Used to be exported and therefore costs, reflecting Activity .

cloud computing deployment models

From the above discussion, it can be said that cloud computing model tat is demand-based services to end users offers. clouds in the physical infrastructure used, where the clouds (Virtual Infra-structure) software used to deliver service to customers are. such infrastructure and middleware in terms of service, administrative areas and meet different users. the establishment the cloud is di-vided into three types, namely: public cloud , private cloud ,hybrid cloud [17].

Public Cloud

Public cloud model is the most commonly used. data Centers made by public cloud providers are quite are large, consisting of thousands of servers with high-speed networks are. These clouds to support thousands of users in the area are public. Public clouds are most popular Google appengine , amazon web Services Microsoft azure during this deployment, public cloud services in a "pay - per - use rates" are available. a public cloud can offer any of the following services: . PaaS , SaaS, IaaS.

Private Cloud

While public clouds are quite welcome and Solutions and imple-mentation of such an infrastructure to reduce costs provides in-formation technology, but there are still scenarios where organizations may wish to own clouds hold to your specific needs to pro-vide. For example, industry many health care and the confidentiality of medical data can not be stored in public infrastructure, maintaining a. thus, private clouds within an organization in order to service the information technology bases for internal users provide. private cloud services, more in control of the making the offer. enhance security and flexibility improve the service for which access is limited to one or several organizations. Such private services, restrictions It is the inability to develop a scaled based on demand provides software for end users, while this (scaled on demand) by cloud services public done. an organization can ma-chines the user needs to buy more, but it does not work public cloud can be done quickly. the rise development combines the advantages of both public and private cloud cloud in organization accessible.

Hybrid Cloud

These clouds are a combination of public and private clouds, but activities and tasks for each of the different clouds will smell of each to be independent of its environment. by combining multi-service cloud, public cloud users the ability to find that the transition to the Stay away from the problems and limitations of the past and make it easier to Security and infrastructure systems are aristocrats. in this Infrastructure and computer models ride on a cloud environment they can be two or three individual or group or public form, but this would be possible with other environments data exchange .

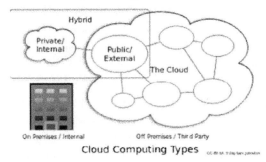

Figure 4: Types of cloud in cloud computing.

From the above we can find out who is trying to cloud computing model with minimal manpower and resources needed to reduce costs and Speed up access to data, answer the needs of users Various fields.

Scope of application of cloud computing

Although cloud computing is not entirely new, but the technology is everywhere is present. over the past few years as quickly Human aspects of life such as education, telecommunications, banking Internet banking services including online bill payment electricity, water and gas ... order online video, online reservation, internet shopping, Internet voice and video calls, chat, Search the web world, social networking and e-mail, games computers, academic research, etc., affect the and especially by a change in the functional areas of management web content, document management, financial management, email management, e-commerce business models in line with the accounting Has evolved. In this section an attempt is the accounting profession in the cloud.

The impact of cloud computing on accounting first

let's be clear that the term accounting. the to achieve this objective a definition of accounting offered.

Definition of accounting

Accounting is called the language of business, because it is through the provision of financial reports, information on economic entities in Stakeholders and interested parties alike. this includes directors, owners, investors, creditors, financial institutions and Such is the state of the economy. [5] From another perspective of accounting, accounting information system called accounting Information system will be remembered that the system Processing of financial information relating to events affecting the organization's business units and reporting of these events is designed for decision makers [1] .accounting, "a statement of basic accounting theory," according to the process of identifying, measuring and reporting financial information to make informed decisions by users of Information. statements mentioned in this definition is followed by Can be "accounting", based on a comprehensive view "Financial information" be considered. [8] In looking at these definitions can be understood that all companies And financial institutions ranging from a small company and institution the country's largest manufacturing plant and accounting information need. for example, if a person is in a Financial investment company does not want to face the situation accounting and finance company knows it. so, to answer if the financial needs of mankind, accounting software was designed.

accounting software application models

Today the use of accounting software pro has three options are: traditional model of software accounting desktop, cloud models and hybrid models.

traditional model

To understand the traditional process models and software applications accounting for traditional desktop computer, consider a company that For all your employees computer and operating system It's different on each install. In this Model for employees, companies should be soft accounting software as a product pur-chased on they and all their computer systems company they put in the hard drive which causes are numerous. why and how? the company has employees usually are files that need to be Interact with each other to process these files, such as a file consider a text report that is due by 5 people edited. one's user? if the company wants the job sharing what to do? So we should give money to install a license on 5 buys a computer and then install it on every single one. first this requires more expensive and, secondly, should the software installation and nearly 5 times if any of the computers should never fail to have a separate Software problems to solve. apart from the need to ensure that all computers have the hardware required to install the software the software has a firmware upgrade to version above shall be considered as if the disk is corrupted members disk, millions of bytes of data in one eye disrupt the disappears. let us examine the issue from another perspective. if Memberships want to edit a text file or picture that you need Software, the software must be purchased and the amount on their computer and then be forced to travel what happens? Can naturally your desktop computer as a result, he never takes the software can not be installed use on any other computer. all of the above, including the costs and constraints of time and place Is applied, the problems that caused the company large and small cloud operating model and accounting services The cloud over them, because it will be the end to the nightmare. Several user instead of installing software on multiple computers, only one run and load the software once and for all people through an online service to which they have access.

cloud operating model

Is currently a hot topic in the world of cloud accounting. accounting cloud, which "Online accounting" they say, like bookkeeping works users are installed on your computer, except that the soft cloud accounting software on the servers' provider online Services ", is applicable to any number of users and companies and organizations can use their web browser, on Internet access it. this means that you as a user company or organization, each time an Internet connection are able to access their company's finances from anywhere and any device you're using. accounting firms and organizations through cloud users online accounting software applications, "presented Software services "in the cloud have access, in fact, the use of accounting software in a similar model (Software as a Service) provider of online services to buy. they for software, hardware or network not pay, but computing power and software services needed to purchase [5]. With this interpretation, if accounting professionals to conclude cloud computing, outsourcing in the old drink New bottles, and many have gone astray. cloud-like Business process outsourcing, such as the purchase of one or more than one offer outsourcing service organization. a key difference in what the buyer is usually a process of outsourcing work is defined as the average salary in what is cloud computing infrastructure and services purchased Fan Some or all of the information that may be do not rely on it. Basically the information technology infrastructure In all areas of business including accounting firms under affects. It seems logical that here the necessity of using cloud computing in accounting to.

operational model combines

Hybrid model consisting of multiple internal and external provider, It is a good option for most businesses, because in This pattern is noncritical and external sources of information in the cloud General processed while the service and the critical control keeps the private cloud have. therefore, organizations can use information technology infrastructure In order to protect their data and efficiently use to keep sensitive information private cloud and anywhere yi automatic scaling up resources needed for public clouds benefit. these resources or services temporarily at maximum load Lease and are then released. 4 -3 need cloud computing model in accounting the first and greatest changes in work organization and will the Internet [12]. Internet changed the way performance businesses and professions upside down, these changes Far beyond e-commerce, because trade a byproduct of the Internet. what caused the change Fundamental processes and culture organizations, the Internet. while the Internet, information technology is the most Responsible for changes in professional practice, has no role Commercial software package Enterprise resource planning systems (Enterprise Resourse Planning) Ignored. Enterprise resource planning systems are doing is all the data are collected in a central source So that access to information is key for members outside the organization much easier. obtain a phase Enterprise resource planning systems will require greater coordination internal system resource planning systems Suppliers and customers, which creates a system resource planning several companies In [20]. enabling technology for the development of such Systems, cloud computing model of the Internet. how technology "here may be, the question is who Information related to the accounting and why the models will need to change? the answer is that investors and creditors as part Professional members are looking for alternate sources of information to assess the performance of the company. while they still have use of the information in financial statements are audited, this information is only available periodically on the basis of past accessibility. therefore, it is reasonable to assume that the expected they are also available for access to key information on the company's internal information systems will be more. this For some people with completely different expectations of disclosures that by The daily for free through sites offering are. It's just a simple financial records and financial statements audited (periodically on the basis of the past), and it available to the public via the Internet, the need for investors ask impatience with current information about the company's financial status are not resolved. Therefore, the information provided for making minor Unless otherwise new model to provide financial information Timely and correct this need to be created and this could be achieved through the cloud computing model. using cloud computing model and the benefits it can make significant progress in achieving Largely through public information data base, especially the Internet as a result, decision makers should be able to Increasingly diverse and timely information for decision-making the. but accounting in computing technologies cloud can be utilized?

accounting of cloud computing technologies

a number of technologies are effective for accounting in the cloud of the: databases (data analysis) expert systems (help deviation analysis, Lending and risk analysis) neural networks (as a tool to predict), storage Information (to provide specific information for users) decision support software (to help decision makers to the data analysis and the impact before a decision to support decisions their choice) superior communication (to improve the accessibility Information) digital signatures and digital certificates (possible Provide continuous auditing). aI-based software (change reports In accordance with the terms possible) data mining and analytical processing time Intelligent agents (in order to analyze information and Contributing to the decision) -1 for data transfer) XBRL re-porting language   2. accounting for the world wide web to facilitate - access to information for investors and analysts, 3- to extract and evaluate the right to use the data S, 4 - Comparison of corporate financial reports. each industry by creating consistency in the classification of financial data) [21]. after considering the nature of the cloud computing model, combining traditional and Necessitates the use of cloud computing technologies in accounting and effective cloud accounting chance has come to two main models Cloud tradition has its advantages and disadvantages compared to the expression Is to determine whether the cloud computing model as a remarkable new technology in accounting or not. 4. Comparison of cloud computing and traditional although cloud computing is an emerging technology in the literature, a lot of work compared with the traditional model of cloud computing that each of the different points on this topic paid. Some

24

researchers believe that the companies to gain application specific software or operating system available Internet or outsource all IT departments Through the use of their IT operations models traditional and entry into new environments by providing Party service providers through the cloud service models.

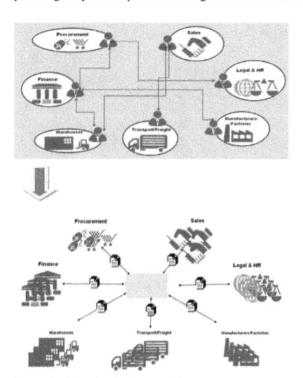

Figure 5 : Operational cloud model

As the images are cloud applications web site is designed for deployment, multiple (To be delivered by a vendor to customer) and users of spatial processing power provided by the seller To share. In the cloud, accounting, and business is business the website is easy to do, in this case you need to buy, Implement and maintain technology infrastructure internal server destroys. unlike the traditional software distribution and has a normal deployment requirements [2]. another difference between the two models is that traditional service providers Their services according to customer's contract offer Long-term contracts are typically one year or more and has properties are relatively constant. but cloud computing service providers, such as water or electricity to provide any level poses qrardard ratio demand services, and the proportion of each service and programs offered charge. however, it assumes you need to use the time in a day, leading to cost reduction For that day. So we can say that the main advantage of cloud computing, reducing Costs for its users.

benefits of cloud computing in Accounting

The benefits of this new technology are: Acceleration time

No doubt if the accounting work using online services and cloud computing can be done, will speed up the letters to people and get them will.

Follow without physical presence

Many times before is that a person is on duty or on leave. If Inter-net-based systems, this one can be in any where it is to communicate via the Internet to letters Respond or refer them to other people.

Connect to other computer systems

Many of the letters the impact on other systems leave office. as for example, a request to leave the system affects the rights and a purchase invoice will affect the storage system over a the impact will affect the reported cost accounting system. thus it can be seen that if a fabric system Using online services, these effects are easily implemented system is.

Availability

Dare to be anywhere today the world where you can find an Inter-net connection. so in If you're using a cloud computing system, none of the employees You are out of your reach and you can easily or part of a purchase order to the officer to another country Prices and specifications are sent or her machine try asking your requirements.

Low-cost computers for users

You need a computer Intensive and thus costly to implement web-based applications you do not need, because the programs are running in the cloud. Improve performance. Since the applications in the cloud are, with few large programs that the computer's memory occupy, users can more performance from your PC See her Increased computing power.

When you work in an environment cloud computing logged on, the power of the cloud and get all the the simple power of a desktop PC is not limited to, but can Functions like a super computer to do and the computer power Server benefit.

Store unlimited capacity building

To the cloud, you have the the system can be connected to the cloud and documents on Heterogeneous systems may no longer be available Note.

Improve matching between documents formats

You do not need to worry about documents that you create on your machine to be compatible with other operating systems and machines. all documents in the cloud by a web-based application is created by the program other cars are also accepted. collaboration easier. sharing documents directly to cooperation The evidence leads. For most users, this is the Users can collaborate on a document or project that is so important Is. It is easily possible with cloud computing.

Universal access to documents

With cloud computing business of any Person (or other document in the document in the computer home office) cell is always avail-able in the cloud. where the document required It was just an Internet connection to connect to cloud computing and the document is available.

Access to the latest version

When you edit a document where Elsewhere, you have access to the latest changes, Because the document is stored in the cloud. Since the total cost for Companies and individuals are important in the cloud computing model, low cost the main advantage is that it can be considered by companies . despite the numerous advantages of cloud computing, it has some disadvantages Is.

disadvantages of cloud computing in Accounting

There are a number of reasons that you may need to remove Not their use of cloud computing. some of the reasons Is as follows:

Requires a constant internet connection

To connect to computing cloud need to connect to the Internet without any access documents in the cloud and there.

Does not work well at low speeds

Now with a contact Low speed is not like a regular phone service computing Cloudy to good use.

Security

Most users rely on cloud computing in accounting concerned Socialization services and security systems and data. all data well and simply stored in the cloud, but there may be data Including confidential files are stored securely in users or Service is disrupted. Therefore, the relevance of socialization computing Cloudy with clear internal controls and audit process [3].

The lack of a comprehensive understanding of control

Lack of control prevailing on the internet cloud systems suppliers, with Issues of data ownership can expose users the higher the risk. So at this point professionals Sas number of audit and accounting should cloud users 70 notify .

Move to cloud computing

It is anticipated that during the InfoWorld news a decade later, it will focus on the world of information technology Its main Internet services (cloud) focus. Statistics show that of previous years and started offering cloud services It was a move towards a more continuous process Clouds there. various reports have confirmed the continuation.

Basic statistics

According to one report, Gartner Group estimates that SaaS sales in 2010 reached Bh9 billion 15.7% increased compared to 2009, and increased $ 10.7 million In 2011, an increase of 16.2% over the year 2010. Gartner Group estimates that well over 10% Sold around the world in applications as SaaS Have. It also estimates SaaS in the world in 2014, more than 16% Applications are included. a report published by the analytical center techmarket view Predicts, the market value of cloud computing in the UK 2010 was £ 5.8 billion in 2014 to 10.4 Billion pound increase.

accounting statistics

LaFollette predicts that in the next 10 years approximately there is no software applications based on the traditional model Found. a recent survey of more than 1,000 companies accounting by - AICPA marketing arm - CPA2Biz Showed that 70% of respondents to increase their use of Web-based applications in the next six to 18 months. planning. As part of the "confidence-building business applications consulting CPA2Biz has negotiated with some cloud vendors". These include companies , copanion, Bill.com XCM and Paychex, Intacct.[2] Russell Evans claims that the current software Cloud-based accounting by a large and growing part of Accountants and accepted two companies, about 14% Companies and 23 percent of accountants (especially young people) in Australian cloud-based software to manage account were self-absorbed. Figure 3: The adoption of cloud computing by accountants and companies [7].

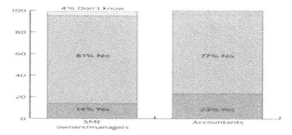

The survey says that 60% of 77% of accountants today cloud systems are not used, probably within the next two to three will do it next year. So, we quickly we are approaching a point where the Cloud accounting software for ubiquitous services that this leads to a large change in the next few years will. the statistics for the accounting profession what could have Is? according to the data, it can be said that the move accountants have not started in the cloud, and your company's business are at risk. therefore, a clear need for accountants are taking the initiative in the solution control their cloud-based clients in your company make the trip with them. thus, the central role management of their clients' accounts are safe and Can again provide strategic consulting services with more value Focus .In the 21st century saw the rise of portable devices tend style for access to Internet services rather than PC are. since such devices and processing facilities are not strong, then who will provide processing power? reply to this the question lies in the cloud. the main driving force behind cloud computing are Include wireless networks, reducing storage costs and improving the software for online processing. with facilities cloud computing cloud service customers will be able to load more inject into your system, reduce costs, experience, new services, and removes unused capacities them. In summary, the following equation is derived cloud. according to the needs of the users of accounting information and the disadvantages of the current model (traditional) application of information technology, determined accounting that eventually led to the timeliness finds. So it is suggested that the accounting system steps in this direction, accounting and security systems audit in accordance with the design and development of new technologies and accounting and financial reporting with the rapid changes in the world keeping the business generated.

Chapter III

Certified System

Since the AI is very muddy, many scholars such as Edward Fig foot in the
1970 Oxford University seeks to resolve the issue of the method is very general and versatile. Researchers found that a specialist is usually a specific styles of work and the order of precedence for the creation of the expert. The last decade saw their desire to take advantage of systems which are called expert systems, largely developed Is. The main difference with other software systems is that expert knowledge processing systems while other applications and data they process. Expert system using knowledge of financial professionals and combining them with modern technology, Of knowledge and expertise to guide decision-making software for individuals Doctors and to implement a significant role in improving decision. Organizing expert fields of different definitions have been proposed, which are mentioned below are some of the refugee definition. Organizing expert fields, fields are computer programs that reflect how an expert in a particular field simulation Hey there. AAA Expert systems are computer programs knows the human thinking process by providing a functional equivalent Experts on a particular issue or task performance, offers. Expert systems, computer programs that use the specific expert knowledge, Yes helps people who are not able to make decisions in complex situations. In fact, The system will recognize them if they had a place experts in the field Believe that expert systems, programs or decided. Software that is adapted to the knowledge of an expert in your store. He is an expert system is a computer program that has the knowledge base Limited in scope and complexity of deductive reasoning wide range of uses to perform tasks Like an expert. The main topic of expert systems, decision making and problem solving. Therefore, systems Certified be composed of two parts: 1. and 2. database engine decision Databases: a mechanism to store information and laws about a topic Is special. - Engine, making it part of an expert system that tries fields of information that people Store, to find an object in accordance with the wishes of the people. Expert system to increase understanding of the above parts such components as: User interface: The interface between the user and the system establishes a connection and allows users Put your question to the system and the ability to interact with the system through This interface is used to restore your answers. This can be as simple as a simple menu interface for entering And exit the dialog or the complexity of natural language, knowledge base: The base of the main System which consists of facts and rules in the field of expert systems and often By legislation in the form of statements "if- then" statement, the control structure: the

31

structure of control The inference engine, also known as the interpreter of the law and the duty to apply and use the information In the knowledge base for solving the problem is, short-term memory: In addition to the knowledge baseWhich is regarded as long-term memory, short term memory is needed to process other Answer and question to answer different path from the hold.

Application of expert systems in Accounting and Finance

Primary assumption in the development of expert systems is that in some areas, a small group of people (Specialists) may work better than the rest of the people featured in the "majority" do, since the knowledge (Specialization) This number is unique, creating a sophisticated system that can obtain the expertise and the Accessible to lay people can improve the performance of decision-making, which This approach assumes, especially in the field of accounting, finance and operations people can This newcomer is professional, provide substantial assistance. accounting and computing and communication needs of the field of computational efficiency by means of advanced reality of uncertainty is inevitable. the instruments used in the accounting system in the last decade Smart PC is that the system is not only used as a computational tool The accountant will be, but as cooperation and consultation as well as helping them solve problems. Today, more extensive use of information technology and constant changes in the processing Information, auditors are faced with new challenges and the importance of validation systems accounting information is added. this is the more complex environment of auditing and accounting requirements as a tool to assist decision-making in this area is greater than ever. Territory of financial issues, including popular areas for the development of expert systems is considered. Nowadays many kinds of expert systems for various applications in the field of finance and accounting are recognized Has been used by several groups, including managers, auditors, financial analysts, Financiers and finally made public. Even experts in various fields And ensure "second guess" the knowledge of the accounting and financial software fo the male to find The financial (accounting and auditing) systems Hey, there's an application of expert systems in the field of financial analysis Below to learn more about this type of application, a variety of expert systems, financial analysis and the definition of their Provided.

Types of financial analysis, expert systems

The definition of financial decision-making process that virtually all of the four data collection, Analyzing, obtaining expert insight and finally decide on the issue involved, the Thus, expert systems are based on the type of service that they offer divided into three types:

1- Helps to gain insight

2- Expert system facilitates decision making

3- Decision systems

In the first of these systems using graphs and ratio analysis, analysis of In the present circumstances. These figures and ratios to those involved in the creation of financial analysis Better insight about the future financial situation and Outlook a useful institution. By doing steps Collecting data, analyzing the decision process is performed by the system. The second system is a knowledge base that can finance the analysis of event ideas Their proposal to the subject of the present analysis that makes it distinct from those systems Be first. Thus, in such systems, three of the four stages of the decision-making process. Application of expert systems in auditing

In the third type of system is the system which are virtually complete financial expert and an expert system Real property, can actually "judge" your special offer. Nowadays, this type Expert Systems with the help of special tools that allow them to produce a result. However, due to problems in the field of financial affairs related to finances based expert systems the help of four groups:

1- Expert system for financial analysis

The main advantage of this system is that the quantitative ratios (such as profitability ratios, Total income, short-term and long-term debt) ratios and qualitative (eg, market position, Organizing employees, business reputation and flexible form of marketing) to be measured.

2- Expert system to analyze the development of commercially successful or unsuccessful In these types of systems: a case study of the development of specific business events before and after using The ability to track the data that have changed over time, analyze and predict its future It is possible to ensure the.

3- Expert system to analyze the market

The system for analyzing sales that have already been produced by the company.

4- Expert system for acquiring knowledge in the field of finance subcommittee This expert system for training managers and other financial professionals used, Of course, prior knowledge of these systems is the ability to quickly develop and However, increasing the incentive to create their own accounting standards and auditing systems Expert. The high standards of the refugee decision-making process more complicated. The Order to promote the success of expert systems increases.

Also, it should be noted Factors such as, lack of training, lack of funding and lack of information sources, it is difficult to determine Suitable application areas, long development cycle systems, the infinite nature of the project and Identifying and expertise to develop the system, the use of expert systems in accounting problems

Organizing expert and auditing fields

Rise of expert systems for effective control of the decision-making process Complex audit has provided a new tool, whereby the audit tasks with ease Much has been done and many solutions to real problems that seem insoluble, Audit lot of its resources in developing and deploying information systems Has invested. Given the complexity of their environment and great judgment, audit treated as a string that the system will go quickly. Design by expert professionals on how to use the knowledge to solve problems Complex, is based. Application of expert systems in accounting and auditing recently and every day The importance of these systems in the field and at the moment of their increasing in many areas Like a lot of planning the audit, evaluation of internal control die, audit, risk analysis, evaluation The entity's internal control, evaluation and control of electronic data processing, analysis, control Enforcement of tax laws and regulations of the Securities Commission, the principles of financial accounting, disclosure Financial analysis and the reporting forms and tasks appropriate to consider the use Is.

Application of expert systems in the evaluation of the continued assumption of unit Examination

One of the most important issues facing the auditor's ability to continue the activity detection unit Be addressed. They should examine the issue of whether, in connection with the continuation of Significantly, the problem is serious or whether it is sufficient to deal with risk management Run. Expert system using knowledge bases (including information regarding the status of other tasks associated. With the same conditions) that they are there, to compare the current situation with the entity Other companies that use them, assuming continuation of the right (wrong), you pay and then The auditor's analysis of whether the usage of this information assumes the continuation of Hamilton is true or not. There are experts in the field of systems auditors It assists in the most important of them are the expert system "expert continuation" Pointed out that the professional knowledge (expert) in areas such as performance appraisal, career, environment Run trading and risk management that can be sustained in the assessment of the entity's auditors. Contribute to more accurate results.

Application of expert systems in the control system to evaluate the entity's internal die

the use of ICT in the process of auditing, partly due to the necessary tasks environments. thus, the clients for information processing increasingly on their internal structure Using the computer and turn the auditors without the use of technologies capable of Reckoning These systems are effective and efficient. moreover, the pressures for cost reduction audit, motivation to find new ways to increase efficiency without reducing the effectiveness of audit to establish the premise, one of these new ways of using expert systems. lehigh internal control evaluation, a critical step in the audit of financial tasks and forms Fields that auditors can demonstrate their skills. acquire sufficient knowledge of the system Client's internal control and risk management assessment is necessary to determine the type above mentioned test, control and management of content and propose new policies and procedures to maintain control the interior is done. In assessing the status of the entity's internal control system design news These systems have been investigating a series of related controls that should exist Offer, also raises questions about the type and characteristics of the entity's controls Asked, then these systems are based on the reviews and comments, appropriate or inappropriate Lehigh existing internal control states. The system can recognize the auditor's expert in this field can help "Internal Control Model" and the auditors noted that an analytical tool in the modeling system Questions about the system of internal control and internal control to assist them in evaluating the internal control system are discussed.

Advantages and disadvantages of organizing expert fields

Advantages of using expert systems for auditors and accountants have many advantages that Such as follows: Increase the availability, lower costs for the user experience, the permanent savings In costs, the reduction of the decision-making problems, multiple experiences, increasing Safety, risk reduction, power, determination, fast response, response in any particular situation, site Experience, user training, facilitate the transfer of knowledge, increase audit efficiency, improve decision-making aid Quality control, training and complex analysis, improve productivity, and so on. Disadvantages: As excessive use of expert systems may be unpleasant results Brought in such fields as medicine, accounting and auditing in the realm of the possible There are serious legal conflicts faced with implementing such systems, and as the amount raised in the court records, the wrong treatment and poor quality product Quickly added. Accountants and auditors as users of the system may

Complaint against together. Thus, it is possible that all individuals associated with expert systems Of the professional manufacturer and developer of information he is legally held responsible. Also, these systems have no sense of what they do and cant do His extensive knowledge of the wider generalization, because for a particular purpose and by Knowledge and expertise that cant be made under the new conditions, unforeseen and analysis Analyze. In today's world, the use of expert systems for analyzing and processing information and access To be more accurate judgments is able to help users make much economic development and increase understanding of the vision. Organizations must take the greatest possible benefit from expert systems, because these systems can help The key business strategies in order to improve performance, follow. The System Certified Human experts can be used in conjunction with the outcome of the decision is based On human expertise and precision machine and also help in uniform do and how to do something. One of the many applications of these systems, the auditing field, In this context, the auditors have provided substantial assistance, depending on their application as a colleague, Residents and experts are employed. The expert system in addition to benefits such as reduced The cost to the user experience, being permanent, cost savings, reduced time to decide Difficult conditions, multiple experiences and increase the reliability, has some disadvantages, such as having a sense of proportion The work done, and not to be extended to the broader generalization of expertise are. Auditors In a wide range of expert systems in areas such as audit planning, activity recognition unit Maturity, understanding of internal control structure, estimate the importance of preparing audit reports are, of course, It should be noted that the auditors did not rely on the results of the expert system, unless the Consideration of other supporting evidence, because the expert system only as a means are auxiliary opinion and responsibility of the auditor's opinion on the audit. Therefore, if the system of Certified Auditors, together with other evidence in their comments, Can make better decisions and appropriate comments.

Chapter IV

IT audit and its definition

Audit of Information technology was first introduced in the mid-1960s. Since then it has had a tremendous advances in information technology have occurred. with the arrival of these new technologies in the field of trade, huge changes in information technology audit coatings. IT audit, IT-based system to help auditors in the process of planning, executing, controlling, and directing the audit is completed. advances in information technology have led firms to conduct trade of new tools such as electronic exchange of data and databases used. In fact, users demand the audit profession has changed and they want to know what the comments are corporate auditors about the reliability of data updates. so we can say that the progress of information technology has increased the demand for IT audit. audit IT audit and audit automatic processing of computer data call. this type of audit, an audit of the electronic data processing is also called. IT Audit, enables auditors to audit issues directly and through modern communication tools to access. In fact, today many companies use different systems for processing electronic data processing accounting data, the only way to check and validate reports, audit information technology. IT audit or audit of information systems, IT infrastructure is a test of controls. In fact, systematic process of collecting and evaluating information technology audit objective evidence supporting one or more claims of the information systems, procedures and operations of an organization. assessment of evidence obtained during the audit shows that information systems are safe, properly maintained and operation data in an efficient organizational goals are met. This type of audit may coincide with the audited financial statements, internal audit, or other forms of accreditation services to be performed. IT audit should not be confused with the financial audit. although there may be some slight similarities exist between the audit, but the goal is primary a financial audit, assess whether the financial statements of a company with accepted accounting principles and standards compliant or not. The main tasks of an IT audit, evaluation of system performance and security programs, especially the ability of organizations to support transmission and distribution assets and correct information between authorized persons. However, the question that arises is that the IT auditor should be what kind of experience? the answer is specialized in the field of IT audit, there is no experience require this type of audit. IT auditors as auditors of the financial or operational start, while others come from other professions IT audit IT. however, the association for information systems audit and Control for IT auditors globally recognized certification as a certified Information systems auditor grants. the title suggests that professionals get past the hard test and gain experience, training and personal competencies, skills needed to do something that they expected to obtain and have. IT audit to be "the process of gathering and analyzing evidence in IT environments to achieve the goals of pre-defined audit" defined. audit objectives vary depending on the nature of the audit. the financial audit, the primary objective of the audit report, an independent report on the integrity and fairness of the financial statements will be audited entity. however, if the activities of the unit so remarkable computerized audit, the auditor should be to what extent the IT system relied on the opinions of professional. of the auditor's procedures and actions to achieve such a comment is assumed, the so called IT auditing. the Information systems audit completely generalized because of the complexity and cost of large-scale information systems. as time goes beyond information-processing computer to perform a task. computers were initially used only in large organizations that charge high prices and exorbitant costs of their operations on coming. the advent of microcomputers and the rapid decline in the price of computer technology, intermediate institutions are also able to use the advantages of computers in processing the data. even in small organizations and small broad access to powerful computers and computer software packages has led to the widespread deployment. as a result, auditors are increasingly faced with the challenge of gathering audit evidence of the IT environment. the large number and variety of risks need to audit the IT people.

a variety of factors related to IT auditing

Professional audit, IT audit have been introduced to different categories, but three regular and special way to carry out an audit of information technology there. First, the audit process of technological innovation. the purpose of this audit, planning is a form of risk for current and future projects. the audit examined the types of technologies used by the company and also to assess the market for these technologies, organization and evaluation of each project component industries of the project or product related organizations, groups. other forms of information technology audit, the audit of innovations. the audit, as the name implies, means of innovation capabilities of audit firms compared to other competitors. this type of auditing, research facilities and research and development company to test and evaluate the evidence supporting the new products generated deals. The third form of IT audit, audit technological status. the audit also technologies that already exist in the companies and technologies that the company needs to achieve it, check. section

404 of the Sarbanes Oxley Act, requires that managers limited effectiveness of internal control systems in their organization over the course of financial reporting and the independent auditors to assess the effectiveness of the systems of internal control requires to verify. due to the increasing use of sophisticated technologies such as enterprise resource management systems by companies, evaluating the effectiveness of internal controls increased use of IT audit procedures need to. (Gelinas et al., 2008) believe that Sachs (2002) the importance of knowledge related to accounting information systems for auditors has increased. similar laws in other countries (such as law firms in Australia and the UK) is responsible for management and auditors with respect to the internal control systems has increased. While Glynas and colleagues (2008) primarily related to the importance of accounting information systems refer to independent auditors, the internal auditors have expressed similar argument could be made, so that the internal auditor's knowledge and expertise can help manage the system organizations to accomplish the sax section 404. I presented the results of a skill set by Bush, broad. although he stated that the level of IT skills are necessary for the auditor to believe that at least 25% of the stated conditions requires an amount of experience. these findings indicate that the IT skills that have been identified by Bush I may auditors IT professionals with different ratings and different experience levels are used. IT audit skills largely because IT auditors to audit and should be in the field of information technology and professional expertise. Information Systems audit and control association, in addition to rigorous testing requirements for certification as an auditor to confirm information systems, having at least 5 years of experience as an imperative. also from an audit perspective, internal auditors that are customary audit compliance, operational and financial organizations do, you may need to have professional expertise in information technology, so that the implementation, operation and maintenance of IT systems in an organization, have the skills. If internal auditors have the skills, you will likely be able to perform IT audits and if unable to do so is not audited by other sectors such as IT (Information Systems Management) have been outsourced or done or jointly outsourcing is complete. thus, we can conclude that the knowledge and technical skills essential for IT audit. substitute for technical knowledge, professional certificates such as certificates of Information Systems Auditor, certified internal auditor or chartered accountant is issued by professional organizations or regulatory. (Tubbs, 1992; Janvrin et al., 2008), for example, evidence from the literature suggests people who have a record chartered accountant or Certified information

systems auditor, they are compared to those without these documents, they will have more progress. (Wier et al., 2000) 85 percent of the jobs auditors are attributed to the in information technology, the need for or professional certificates are to be preferred to have the documents and certificates, or the way work is required to obtain these documents. this evidence suggests that the relevant professional certification such as certified Information Systems auditor or certified Internal auditor or certified management accountant, is directly related to IT auditing. but as previously mentioned, in addition to IT auditors specialized IT knowledge, skill sets needed for financial audit. information systems audit and control association of additional skills and knowledge that is responsible for the certification audit, information systems, information systems auditor certification test are more related to time spent internal auditor by the audit information is. but since the certificates certified Internal auditor and certified management accountant general nature (eg the certification audit, information systems tend to have fewer IT), IT audit them regularly and not associated with the rule. topics related to professional certificates, continuing professional education as an important factor to prepare for audits of internal audit at the same time as the IT audit. continuous professional training in many professional organizations (such as the American society of certified public accountants, Institute of internal auditors) a requirement to maintain professional certification. for example, the institute of Internal auditors standards require that Internal auditor shall be 24 months, 80 hours of training. but probably the only part of continuing professional education that focuses on information technology, for internal auditors to audit information is useful. Internal audit, IT audit is directly related to age. some researchers believe that the audit senior managers in determining the duration of the assignment given to the various types of audits, including audits information technology, power and influence are more likely to be experienced audit Senior managers, who are interested in serving more time on traditional audit to audit IT. other factors linked with IT audit, the size of the organization. larger companies may spend more time IT audit to smaller companies. the auditors who have a bachelor's degree or higher, compared to those who were undergraduate students, more time was spent on IT auditing. In this paper, the use of the literature, factors associated with IT audit by internal auditors identified. certified information systems auditor's findings show a direct relationship with the IT audit. therefore, it is reasonable to conclude that an increasing number of professionals in the information systems auditor internal auditor certification, resulting in a corresponding increase in IT audit will. certifications, certified Internal auditor and certified management accountant, an important relationship with their IT audit, IT audit is inversely related to the CPA certification. since many of the organizations internal auditors from the candidates certified accountant or other expert employ certificates, the question is whether, considering the inverse relationship between certification and audit conducted chartered accountant, certified chartered accountant with more and more information systems auditor should be employed under whether for more investigators are needed to answer this question. another finding is that education at the basic level or at the level of expertise is directly related to IT auditing. research also indicates a direct effect on the internal auditor audits the age of information technology. internal auditor older, more time is spent on IT auditing. finally, a similar topic for future studies could examine the differences in IT audit by various industries. For example, one would expect the IT audit by the internal auditor in technology companies, the larger of the audit in government departments.

Chapter V

Topics of artificial intelligence

artificial neural model components that have a direct resemblance to real nerve components. This model was first raised McCullough and Pitts input symptoms that are continuous variables. Each can accept input values affects certain weight. The processing elements (neurons) will have two parts. The first part of the weighted inputs together and I called entity to acquire; The second part is a nonlinear filter that is usually called the activation function which is determined by the output. Among the factors that influence as a continuous variable (such as different values in an interval between different companies) are considered They are the past returns of stocks, the price of the stock, the price of the coin, the price per barrel of crude oil and so on. The weight for each input channel is considered that the true extent of its impact on the future price (Estimated price) shows. Below are a few of the possible active function is shown. The activation threshold is a function that can be crossed only information I have is that the output of the first artificial nerve is the value of T exceeds the threshold. It can also function as a function of the signal when the output is less than the threshold T send negative information. When the output is greater than a threshold value T is positive information to send. In most cases, the activation function is a continuous function such that the function or sigmoid function is called. The most commonly used activation function, the logistic function is to activate a variety of functions such as S is between zero and one is a horizontal asymptote. α is the ratio of the change in function between the two asymptotic values, the slope of the function specifies. Because of the nonlinear functions are used in artificial nerve is that we can create extra nonlinear modeling. Artificial Neural Networks as an artificial intelligence techniques seek to mimic The functioning of the human brain. An artificial neural network is part of a large number of nodes and lines Loaded The nodes are connected to each other is formed. Sensor nodes are nodes in the input layer and The output layer nodes, nodes are called to respond. Nero final between input and output neurons Are hidden. The input layer is a layer of neural computing nodes because it does not have the weight of the input activation function. One of the most important features that the teeth Artificial Neural Networks Closer to the people, the power of learning. Networks Nervous to learn to follow all of the rules defined by human experts, the rules of evidence) such as input-output relations (often used. It is one of the most important benefits Neural networks than traditional expert systems. Artificial neural network learning, unlike traditional statistical methods, the default attributes of the data distribution is independent of the input variables are not.

Propagation neural network method can be used for any number of layer The middle of the country. The purpose of learning is that the weights are adjusted so as to present a collection of pictures yha, good teeth to come out. It is a network with a large number of input-output examples Jhay Zhu called, are taught. Training methods are as follows: 1. Select weights to small random numbers (both negative and Positive) 2. Input a couple of sets of educational training Choose 3. Enter the input and output vectors to compute network See, 4. the margin of error (the difference between the network output and the desired output) to Calculate 5. diverse network weights adjustment that error At least, the 6 steps 2 through 5 for each pair of training Repeat the training set where the error as Acceptably low. Characteristics of neural networks of other branches of AI or computational methods traditionally distinguished as follows: Learning by example: As we said couples Input for use of the network. Ignore its flaws, so you can use a neural network Input data used for distorted or confused. Are able to recognize the pattern. The use of parallel processing because different aspects Consider a pattern here. Low energy consumption: based on parallel processing and neural network Privacy learned, consumes little energy. Aristotelian binary logic or fuzzy logic to everything Only two of the black and white, yes and no, zero, one sees the There. And it is logical that in the range of zero And a set of zero or one, and only if the absolute value of belonging to a member of the A. For example, a 40-year 15% of the youth And 70% of adults and 25% of the collection Say that they do not belong elderly and middle-aged (The sum awarded is not necessarily equal to one). Fuzzy Logic in 1965 for the first time Article of the same name, Professor Lotfi Zadeh presented. . Fuzzy logic is a new technology that extra conventional way For the design and modeling of a system that requires Using advanced mathematics and relatively complex The amount and terms of the language, or in other words Expert, and aims to simplify and streamline the system design Replace or largely completed in the premise. One feature Fuzzy logic is flawed and illogical entries with The use of such laws (if ... then ...) to answer certain Brings. The two-stage fuzzi fication (conversion process is to format numbers and Data Fuzzy numbers, phrases or words on the production process A consequence of quantifiable) in this process within Be Repetition algorithm based on genetic algorithm and its basics Adapted genetics. These algorithms on various issues such as Optimization, identification and control systems, image processing issues, combined, Set topology and training artificial neural networks and systems. Based decision rule is used. Repetition algorithm based on genetic algorithm and its basics Adapted genetics. These algorithms on various issues such as Optimization, identification and control systems, image processing issues, combined, Data set topology and training artificial neural network and systems Based decision rule is used.

Genetic Algorithm

1. Create a population of random strings: string form (Chromosome) in the event that the number of tasks associated with We highlight each variable and the sum of the number To get. The City by the length of the number of bits forming Time. Although the sequence of bits corresponding to a particular variable And the status of each variable in the process of genetic algorithm is fixed. Each potential solution to the problem is to be provided by a string. 2. Evaluate each string in the population. Assessment of the value function as a liaison between the algorithms Genetic optimization problem of the act. Value function for Each string is assigned a value that is proportional to the ability to respond Which is expressed by the string. For many problems, especially Function optimization problems, the value can be easily The fitness function is measured by the value of the objective function The user defines. 3. Select the parent: This process, however, randomized, But any parent who is elected directly proportional odds With its elegance. The worst part of the population may be able to However, this algorithm is selected by the process of this algorithm There is also an element of randomness. However, after several Generation, the members of the population are excreted. 4. A new strand exchange and mutation operators Create: Exchange operator: There are several types, but the most famous is the exchange operator They exchange operator has a point. In this case, if the test, Give permission to share a random number between one and during the course of production Will. Mutation: the use of the operator's ability to Genetic Algorithms To find near optimal solutions that oral administration increased. The method is applied to This means that for each element of a sequence, test, Mutation occurs. If the test is successful The amount of from one to zero or zero to a change The attributes that do not exist in the parent population, creating Are. Unlike exchange mutation probability is low. 5. Members of the population to create space for new fields to delete, 6. Evaluates new field, put it into the new population. 7. If you have stopped all the time back in the field Otherwise, return to step three. Termination test algorithm for detecting the stop of practices Psoriasis can be used. For example, we can converge The total population is taken into account (or any part of the field, all alone Variables show). Restore discipline to the set of variables

(decoding) for the the objective function value and therefore it is necessary to assess the degree courses The variables to be converted. For this purpose a number of bits for each Variables, types of variables (continuous or discrete) and the location of each variable in Is specified. Further, in the case of artificial intelligence applications in accounting and Finance and research is carried out. It is worth mentioning that the Mentioned are only a sample of the investigation.

Application of Neural Networks

Predict the trend of stock prices:

Forecast price or return on equity was not easy, because many market factors involved in determining That all these factors can not be merely technical analysis (only Historical Data on the price movement and trading volume To predict the future movement of the price) considered . Thus it is proved that the use of more sophisticated computational tools and algorithms such as neural network acting Synthetic modeling of nonlinear processes that result in the price of the stock, the better responses statistical methods to lose.

Audit: ANN can be used in the audit process Decision analysis helps sustain other activities

Predict the amount of credit:

Artificial neural system may be different from that of the input data to the Data Customer Data desired output and the actual decisions Analysts Credit. The system aims to mimic the human decision maker in granting Or rejection of credit and credit ceilings. Another advantage of the ANN forecasting model is linear That can be applied to a broader set of Financial Data and need not require assumptions such as linearity and normality. Kumar has conducted a study that compared the effectiveness of non-linear fashion   Lehigh linear fashion forecast financial ability to pay was explained teeth.

Estimated cost

When estimating the cost of many factors, including the constantly changing nature of technology, availability of materials and wages Direct and currency values, etc. should be considered. Therefore, given the high input data are incomplete and sometimes neural network can be a good option for the estimated cost.

Application of Fuzzy Logic

 Decision:

Among the applications of fuzzy logic in decision-making that can use the values of the time, in teeth Uncertain as to give definitive answers. In today's changing and uncertain environment, strategic decisions are very complex in nature and fuzzy. have also carried out a study of fuzzy logic to shape decisions about new product features.

Audit

Fuzzy logic and fuzzy sets can be measured in terms of auditors and audit risk and uncertainty management in the audit environment, help. For example, when the auditors state that certain internal controls are effective internal controls are in a fuzzy set. Therefore, given the nature of the auditor's work, there seems to be a potential factor that will audit the use of the theory of fuzzy relation.

Application of Genetic Algorithm

Prediction of bankruptcy:

Bankruptcy is a very important global issue with high social costs. So It is important to predict. To solve the problem of bankruptcy, the researchers used a set of rules or conditions have been obtained using the GA. Based on these conditions, the model will predict whether or not a company is faced with the possibility of bankruptcy. For example Lnsbrg (2006), who has done research for bankruptcy 28 potential variables that previous research material have been diagnosed, genetic programming is used. As a result, six variables were identified as important.

Combined Application of Artificial Intelligence

ABC

Traditional ABC reasons may distort the price of finished products. Among these reasons are: First, the general criteria for selecting a cost-driven ABC 20 is not relevant. Second, when the cost of a non-linear relationship shows, ABC is a linear relationship between the activities and the allocation of indirect costs into consideration. To solve these problems, we can use a combination of artificial intelligence techniques. for example, Kim and Han (2003) in their investigation of the genetic algorithm to identify the drivers of cost-optimal or near-optimal use. In addition, the artificial neural network to allocate indirect costs to the nonlinear behavior of the product is used. Undertaken concluded that the model works better than the traditional model.

Prediction of bankruptcy

Keenan (2004) feature a neural network model to predict bankruptcy company Using information obtained from the forms of financial tasks examined. Network structure and its input was selected by the genetic algorithm. The model was compared with the LDA model. The results showed that bankruptcy is predictable, and also the mixed model of neural networks and genetic algorithms better than the model, LDA The scope of works (Keenan, 2004). Kumar and Ravi (2007) have conducted a study, a comprehensive review of the work during the years 2005-1968 in the intelligent application of statistical techniques to solve difficult to predict which companies and banks facing bankruptcy offers them.

Predicting stock prices

artificial neural network model for this purpose, the ability to efficiently develop a reasonable time not. On behalf of Fuzzy logic approach also needs to learn from the experiences of others is so successful combination of these two approaches, has been the subject of many studies.

Audit:

Lane and others (2003) conducted a study employing fuzzy neural network to detect fraud 22 Review concluded that the FNN The study further improve the statistical methods and artificial neural networks has been reported in previous studies acts. Lenard (2001) of a hybrid system is used to determine the continuity of activity. All relationships between the variables in the model, artificial intelligence, and many have not discovered that some discovered and proven industrial section, the terms. The results of artificial intelligence model, provided sufficient data and design are almost the best. However, most AI research in accounting bookkeeping is done by researchers and experts AI is not much help. If accounting researchers and practitioners work together AI, AI research in accounting will improve. Because researchers AI, the key to solving some particular cases of the general accounting Auditing through techniques such as fuzzy logic, neural networks, and other areas of AI, which previously was not used in accounting. Important audit work is complex and poorly done it with devastating results and thus make use of as much of the AI of the people.

Chapter VI

Artificial intelligence applications in different areas of Finance

In this section, the areas of financial management and investment suggests that the artificial intelligence tools are have been used extensively, certainly, in this paper, it is not fully explain topics them. the reader is informed that the aim is simply proportional to the area of financial activities, can help if they need to have systems in place to work. financial simulation: the financial structure of the business operations, complex and dynamic. although the duties of a financial manager can be components, sub-divided, but the interrelationships between these smaller subtasks still very complicated. help special specific models that are tailored to the financial structure over time companies maintain their dynamic and responsive relationships with other sectors of the financial modeling and non-financial corporations and international organizations are. for example, we can construct a neural network model of consumer credit behavior with changes in economic conditions simulation. the input data can involve the general economic information and specific information about customers and output data patterns can buy or pay the customers. the teaching model of data customers can use the previous behavior. Such a system for planning and expenditure for doubtful accounts seasonal fluctuations in the valuation of accounts receivable and credit and credit ceilings for different clients, very useful. for fund management, capital project evaluation, risk management assets and personal property, rate risk management equality, and the anticipated cost of credit and availability of funds can be used for simulation. three areas the following is the main:

Predict the future

however, in some areas, financial forecasting, computer software and traditional, more optimal network models neural and hybrid instruments. especially if we have known models of computing seek, in this cases, the use of traditional computer-effective and logical models. but financial analyst in more concerned about the impact of specific actions on the behavior of investors. in this case, the model does not have a defined relationship. investors based distributed information about the company, its not respond. all data are also influenced by the various resources of the company to reach them. build a simulation model that investors react to changes in dividend policy, accounting methods, reported earnings, capital structure, or any other issue or increase capital stock splits meet. education such a model that estimates of real investors and the documented information is used. studies the last of these, mainly to assess the reaction of investors to rely on changes in stock prices, but investors other than buy or sell, other reactions show. artificial neural system can be used as a financial analyst the increase in the reaction of investors to predict changes in corporate financial policy. model that are designed this way, alternative models that, in the framework of statistical methods were designed. using linear regression techniques or polynomial regression on their own, moving averages, and even baks-models to predict financial jenkins has been common. now, many tests have proven that using neural networks to respond better statistical methods leads up .

Evaluation

Using neural network models and hybrid models, the value of securities and other assets are we buy, we estimate. in this case, we must simulate human evaluation process in neural network Imitation may be the most important.

Credit approval

Although the task of credit ceilings, especially in the case of consumer credit, the staff and institutions of lower level managers financial transfer, but now it's time for the user. elements of quantitative and subjective decision-maker obscures range. in addition, more information on the basis of their decision to take the final decision to grant credit in the form official data that have a specific format, not him. artificial neural system can be taught in such a way that the input data and customer data the desired output is the real decision credit analysts. target system to mimic the human decision maker grant or the validity of credit ceilings. there is no need for the information system can be thrown in a specific format, the input data are varied and sporadic use. functions of neural system, the financial implications of this paper, the main work of the class classified information. the classification of new cases according to their similarities with the patterns in the model memory. what we said in the previous paragraph are the functions of forecasting and modeling. in most applications, the net financial nervous-looking model, the search continues for pattern recognition. financial signal processing function is still not much use (unless the owners voice identification documents such as credit cards) and these models are better ways to detect signs of such classification for sound.

Financial institutions

financial institutions, the transfer of money in the financial markets and monetary policy through a significant impact the performance of the economy. three main financial institutions, ie banks, savings institutions and investment intermediaries investment by reducing transaction costs and reducing information costs, financial markets will lead to effective action [19].

Bankruptcy evaluation (assessment of risk lending)

What about the credit rating of the above mentioned, the lending institutions will use commercial and consumer loans. financial institutions can also help in the study of artificial neural systems and the decision on the loan request payment or non-payment of their decisions. however, these systems do not take the final decision on large loans, In this case, at least in terms of the system output can be considered an expert.

Asset management and securities portfolio

Financial institutions will have a number of stocks, bonds, mortgages, real physical assets such as land their choice. the risk adjustment, the supply markets, the effects of the tax, and the deadlines, and many other variables should the decision be taken continuously. managers types of investment funds and investment banks should their decisions. the task becomes more difficult when you consider that the economic and financial environment is constantly fluctuating, a. due to the nature of unstructured decision processes portfolio manager and the uncertainty of the economic and financial situation and scattering data, an appropriate arena for the implementation of neural network models emerge. on the other hand, the professional investors have to say, given the circumstances of each investor's holdings, time horizon, risk and cash flow mode of a different opinion. the management of such assets to determine these variables the risk is minimal and maximum efficiency. different classes of assets including currencies, bonds (bonds), stocks, insurance life, cash, real estate, gold and decorative objects, cell phones, vehicles and the like are all kinds of deposits in banks risks and returns that are different from each other. until now, many models have been proposed to solve the problem of optimal asset each year according to the Initial plans have limits on this model using quadratic programming was introduced. but if there are too many variables in this model was faced with the problem of computing. the following specialists using methods such as creating a single index, the mean absolute deviation and data envelopment analysis, attempts to convert it to have a linear method. others also other models such as the non-linear model, artificial neural network (working class classified information), model making, planning and dynamic programming to solve their problem. although these models are solved in theory but in practice the methods of mathematical programming problems in this area there are. the nature of risk measures to prevent the creation of a general solution becomes too general methods of solving nonlinear problems due to the non-convex objective function can not be used in addition to the normal size selected issues of assets in the real world contains hundreds of assets that return and risk of the assets using the series time comes. thus, given the large size of the optimization problem is solved with software packages commonly used in problem solving. mathematical programming is not possible. investment managers act as constraints on the optimization of their assets actions that caused this problem becomes more complex due to the problems existing in the model solution nonlinear programming problem of assets, other researchers in mathematical programming techniques are used to solve the problem. the "meta-heuristic methods for solving optimization problems are considered and many researches in this field is. in particular, genetic algorithm was widely used as an efficient search .

Pricing of new issues

Financial institutions in countries with developed capital markets, the pricing of new issues are responsible. this pricing is a complicated process that has a direct impact on the company's rate of return. In the first panel prices in Tehran stock exchange has always been problematic and is the subject of much controversy. information about the issuer may be incomplete, non-standard forms of information provision, and only a short time period will be included. information relating to the same company and the same industry, as well as information on current and future economic conditions should be considered. in addition, a subjective element in his work to the degree of acceptance of the investor and the rate of interest to be measured and appropriate time for the new securities issue to be determined. here again, the neural network can be trained so that the decisions of human experts through all data and actual outcomes of decisions taken in the past, emulate. in addition, in this environment, the system has the potential to improve the performance of a human expert, because the input data can include the price changes actual sales activities later on the issue of securities. the system has the potential to directly from the decision maker human and the actual results obtained from the decisions, learn. in addition, such a system could even leave the company by a human expert to continue to serve, and thus gained valuable experience and expertise is immortal.

Financial markets and investment professionals

Financial markets, informal and organized market in which the transmission funds from individuals and units that are faced with surplus funds to individuals and entities seeking funds(resources) are place. obviously the majority of lenders in the market and the majority of applicants for funds to households and firms the state form. financial markets needed to transfer the savings of natural and legal persons and other persons the opportunity to have productive investment and financial resources are required to provide. artificial intelligence applications in the critical areas of financial activity that has the task of transferring funds directly, in other sectors are described. as one can see in the table, often artificial intelligence tools in the management portfolio of securities, transaction projections and estimates and advice to help employees come to this area. professional investors the set of arbitrage opportunities, technical analysis, fundamental analysis, evaluation of investment projects and so the tool are strong artificial intelligence. various financial areas in which expert systems are used, because of the importance of the area described separately are given.

Insurance: Certain applications in the industry is concerned, include

purchase commitment: expert systems can be used to more coherent institutional standards for assessing the degree of possibility of different hazards (fire, flood, theft, etc.) has increased. knowledge base purchase obligations include specific information about the systems of industrial safety equipment and measures taken to reduce the level of risk and risk assessment techniques. perhaps the best time to design computer systems in the field, the renewal of insurance policies, because at that time very much in a machine-understandable there. savings of: of how much the current earnings should be possible to claim compensation for the near future had an important question. expert systems in this case can be considered as a tool for allocation comprehensive and coherent response to demands from unknown sources used.

audit: internal audit resources are limited, so insurance companies will need to use these resources use. to limit the scope of the business firms are geographically dispersed and diverse terms of activity, exercise adequate control. the audit involved a very small elements and solutions supplied by traditional systems of the problems it can do.

Banking

banks are also various consumer loans, mortgages, and credit limit to offer their customers. to the In addition, transfers and funds transfer services, the purchase and sale of foreign exchange and other banking transactions can be systems certified used. systems consulting foreign currency that can be qualitatively different market conditions, different strategies and methods to hedge the foreign currency option other assessments and recommend solutions. such systems are often complex analytical tools that currency arbitrage operations can be evaluated and alternative trading strategies under different conditions of the market.

Residents deals

to rely on expert system technology, systems trading tuesday my assistants, bonds, derivative securities and exchange is established. unfortunately, little information is available on the system, which is why designers or owners because they do not speak of them talking advantage of this system is weakened their competitive.

Analysis of financial statements multinationals

Multinational companies have unique problems of reporting and compliance with the law. currently, these companies should approach the problem of instability such as different forms of reporting, legal requirements and forms of their accounts buckle. expert systems have greatly reduced the problem. they have the same approach to help institutions to adopt a standard financial statement analysis. the expert system configuration information such as accounts, balance sheets and profit and loss statements using the basic analysis that has been done on domestic enterprises, analyzes. this standard makes the differences between the financial reporting in different countries will be removed. Presented in each of the basins of financial management and investment, with the help of various technologies, artificial intelligence, great deal of research has been done. result of the application of artificial intelligence systems can be no doubt that the industry financial services, has made great development and the trend will continue. expert systems are used in cases where there is a huge amount of data, whereas neural networks artificial intelligence and fuzzy logic in such a complex, ambiguous and incomplete various aspects of the subject, there is a lack confidence in the face area, are more efficient. genetic algorithms, with the help of their unique benefits considerable optimization problems and classify and integrate it with other tools is always of interest to researchers. finally, we can say that the combination of artificial intelligence tools always gives better results.

Chapter VII

Information Technology

The use of IT in business and industry. in other words, the purpose of information technology, mechanical or electrical equipment is in production and will be used to build more efficient systems. evolution of IT technology, including the administrative, computer technology and communication technology. in the first period, employers were trying to create an environment that is separate from the general problems of factory production environment, all administrative, staff and business is done. the most prominent feature of this period, studies on housing and office space for the environment. In fact, in the course of trying to separate the administrative activities of manufacturing activities and the staff of the spatially separated from the operating units. it was thought that a better environment for administrative affairs be provided at that time, most of the computing such as accounting, payroll and finance. in the second period, the period of computer technology, with the arrival of a small computer with speed and precision, the directors decided to using this device and your computer speed and accuracy of the computer and remove errors in the reduction of working time and human consequences of this move was that the computer will help users to perform daily activities as well. in the third period, the period of communications technology, with increasing and widespread use of computer technology and its peripheral devices and system integration and integration of each of the others arose. in fact, today, office systems and global systems that their main task is to create relationships and improve communication. typically, the communication of business information is of great importance. another characteristic of this period except in they are living, is that of hower companies have realized the true value or quality of the information.

The role of information technology in entrepreneurship

With the features and capabilities of information technology has caused considerable flexibility in the field of entrepreneurship. this feature increases the performance of these technologies have been employed in the creation of jobs. some of these features include: 1) speed: calculation and processing information quickly and immediately transfer it to reduce time and thus increase productivity. IT search and quick access to information it provides. 2) increased accuracy: jobs based on human variable precision work, while information technology, high accuracy and ensures a constant supply. the types of computer processing and computational accuracy far more than human. 3) reduce the physical size of data repositories: the development and deployment of information technology, it is no longer necessary to transport and store large volumes of reference books there are specialized and easily at any compact disc, save the information or the resources of several books having received via computer networks. 4) elimination of administrative corruption: the use of information technology to increase transparency in doing things by removing many of the key advantages. this leads to the elimination of administrative corruption are especially at low levels.5) Create the possibility of full-time work: IT support, information and referrals, many people and so on through computer networks is done automatically. twenty-four hours so it can be utilized. 6) the ability to work remotely: telecommunications, telephony, conferencing and collaboration systems, electronic exchange of data, examples of applications of information technology in this field. 7) reduce the cost of the system or by based on the foregoing, especially speed, which makes more work to be done and doing the work of all time, increases system efficiency and thus reduce the amount of the costs. as mentioned make remote collaboration is a feature of IT. taking advantage of the skills telecommunication and communication efficient and desirable, employees can plan their work as they are in the office of follow another place like that are present in your workplace, some professionals on problems and opposition available for effective use of information technology and human resources have been overcome and the way to convince executives organizations have achieved great success. the reality is the product of 10 hours to 10 hours in the office, home, clearly notice that working at home is much more qualitative and quantitative terms, was higher. the things that you need to sit in one place and focus, such as the development and improvement of budgetary analysis salary of employees, develop policy and procedures can be done at home. it must be admitted that the "remote" to do any task cant always optimal efficiency and may be useful in practice. however, in practice it may not be applicable to an entire office hours during the day, month and week at home Sit and do their work because there is always the need for dialogue and the expert meeting on advisory facing colleagues and authorities, and the presence of some issues to resolve. however, IT professionals, executives, and even those who are important tasks and heavy administrative burdens you can sit in your house by taking advantage of information technology and its tasks properly and then the tools in the field of information technology (computers and other tools) the results of its activities to the transfer. if the director of the organization, project management skills, manpower and relationship between the two is whether there is a reason not part of the human resources of its location and use of information technology to properly perform their duties. the question is whether this particular job, including jobs that the employee can perform tasks themselves at home. no, Instead, the question must be asked whether this particular job, or an employee of a number of days work week instead of being at the office, at home, keep your things properly or even do better at home. the reason that some job applicants, scientific and practical information through e-mail sent to the hiring company. probably when they are asked to perform some of the tasks of the residence, they may feel more comfortable. although it is possible that human resources can work remotely, but it is clear that for all occupations, they cant be a solution suggests Some jobs, such as employee or expert on the go need to be discussed and referred not to say that the person is at home with someone else in your organization issues among his leave. for example, employees of the "employee relations" of necessity which at the time was working in the office, since employees usually the problem and get your questions answered in the office "employee relations" refer to these clients say the employee should solve your problem and respond to your home home video via e-mail or communicate with them.

Application of remote work in organizations

When an organization is considering the wishes of their employees during the week or month, days to stay at home and part of his official duties at home first, they must train all staff in the organization and implementation by all employees share this goal. the fact that the commute from home to office and back in some congested areas, the basic problem the staff is. Some workers have to travel in the middle of the day just by spending 30 minutes travel time in busy hours in the morning and the end of the three-hour time period, and the administrative burden for this category the staff are a nightmare come tomorrow because every night the tomorrow to 1/5 hour for the administration and1/5 hour drive back home. the staff are skyrocketing rates of rent in the city have their offices in the city's proximity to live up to pay less rent. they could instead of 3 hours of their time in the home, office and home office hours to spend on personal matters and entertainment and respectively. the advent of information technology and its application to the problem of a large number of employees who wish to apply using "remote" are largely solved. If the work is required and they can stay at home and work permit in your home using a computer and communication equipment to do. but some of the staff of the do not get your inner satisfaction and expectations. when an employee is out of the office environment, the administrators of the will not work during the day and as the environment changes, the organization not all of these factors makes this group of employees not progress. thus, according to the circumstances, employees tend to be "remote" to they have typically employed by organizations to adopt the culture of this type what's employment level executives within the organization and what a way to understand and to accept it.the first step of the staff to evaluate your goals, it is the reasons for this choice (ie, work from remote) for his batting and one reason only, because there is not enough specific reason, sometimes not conducive to the success or the failure to provide a decision. make information systems more efficient and effective use of information and communications technology achievements in the organization and how to communicate quickly and effectively with the devices covered by, the centers for scientific - research country society civil and stakeholders something very serious. make information systems more efficient and effective use of information and communications technology achievements in the organization and how to communicate quickly and effectively with the devices covered by, the centers for scientific - research country society civil and stakeholders something very serious. Failing that the organization not only disrupts the flow of the current affairs of the hive, but the organization's handling of the goals and missions are also open. therefore, appropriate methods for the issues related to the deployment of information systems and their interaction is a serious matter for the organization, it should be noted, information technology as a tool to supplement the however, its use leads to increased efficiency and cost savings and speed and create paperless office systems, etc., from another dimension brought together on the same documents and folders to a computer or printer and a slight increase unimportant messages and wide spread the message of the email. today, information technology tools such as computers, internet and email telegraph etc. achievement is provided for employees who can work in the areas of engineering, design, finance, etc. without although the objective is to manage the tasks at home, do your own work and results through existing systems to transmit the computer centers. the group of accountants and auditors are also subject to such facilities. hope to accelerate due to the rapid developments in information and communication technologies on the one hand, and the rapid pace of developments environment on the other hand, excessive delays in this regard to the interest of the organization and systems, rebuild and forget let us not; "optimum utilization of manpower and improve efficiency can play a decisive role in achieving the goals of the organization."

References

1.Abdul Rahman, A. R. (2003) Ethics in accoun IIUM Journal of Economics and Management 11, no.1, 2-8.

2.Acharya,V.,Pedersen,L.,(2005).Assetpricingwithliquidityrisk.JournalofFinancialEc onomics77,375–410.

3.Bushman,R.,Piotroski,J.,Smith,A.,(2004).WhatdeterminescorporatetransparencyJou rnalofAccountingResearch42(2),207–252.

4.Bushman,R.,Smith,A.,(2003).Transparency,financialaccountinginformation,andcor porategovernance.EconomicPolicyReview9(1),65–87.Bushman,

5.R.,Smith,A.,(2001).Financialaccountinginformationandcorporategovernance.Journa lofAccounting&Economics32(1–3), 237–333.

6.Demsetz,H.,Lehn,K.,(1985).Thestructureofcorporateownership:causesandconseque nces.JournalofPoliticalEconomy93,1155–1177.

7.DeYoung,R.,Flannery,M.,Lang,W.,Sorescu,S.,(2001).Theinformationcontentofanke xamratingsandsubordinateddebtprices.JournalofMoney,CreditandBanking33,900– 925.

8.Diamond,DouglasW.,(1984).Financialintermediationanddelegatedmonitoring.Revie wofEconomicStudies51,393–414.

9.Pyatt.G.;Roe,A. (١٩٧٧)Social Accounting for Development Planning, CambridgeUniversity Press.

10.Pyatt, G.; Round, J. I. Social Accountin 9 Matrices, Symposium Series,Washington D.C.: World.

11.Pyatt, G.(١٩٩١) "Fundamentals of Social Accounting," Economic System Research, 3,pp. 315 - 41.

12.AICPA, (1988). "The Auditor' Consideration of an Entity's Ability to Continue as a Going Concern."Statements on Auditing Standards, No. 59.

13.Darlington, K. (2000). "Designing Explanation Styles for Expert Systems Information". Technology and Communication New Millennium Conference, Bangkok Thailand, August.

14.Dowling, C. (2009). «Appropriate audit support system use: the influence of auditor, audit, and firm factor». The Accounting Review, No. 3, pp. 771–810.

15.Oleary, E. D. and P. R. Watkins (1989). "Review of expert systems in auditing". Expert systems review. Spring, pp. 3-22.

16.Hagan, J. M., Mark, A. and D. K. Schneider (2002). "Using a neurofuzzy expert system to address ambiguity problems in dept/equity issues of closely held corporations". Academy of Accounting and Financial Studies Journal, No. 1, Volume. 6, Issue. 1, pp. 1-7.

17.Meduffie, R. S. and L. S. murphy (2007). "Impact of an audit reporting expert system on learning performance". Journal of Accounting Education, No. 1, Vol. 15, pp. 89–101.

18.Metaxiotis, K. S., Psarras, J. E., D. T. Askonis (2002). "Genesys: an expert system for production scheduling". Industrial management & data systems, No. 6 (9), Volume. 102, pp. 309-317.

19.Morgan, B. (2002). "the impact of expert system audit tools on auditing firm in the year 2001, a Delphi investigation". Journal of Information Systems, No, 7 (1), Spring, pp. 16-34.

20.Phillips, M. E. (1991)." Expert systems for internal auditing". Internal Auditor, No.1, pp. 1-9.

21.Rada, R. (2008).'' Expert systems and evolutionary computing for financial investing". Expert Systems with Applications,No. 34, pp. 2232–2240.

22.Sbalen, R. M. and S. Schrader (2007)."Collection, stovage and application of human knowledge in expert systems development". Expert Systems, No. 5(11), Vol. 24, pp. 346-355.

23.Svinze, A., Kran, V. and U. S. Murthy (1991). «A generalizable knowledge-based framework for audit planning expert systems». Journal of Information Systems, No. 5(2), pp. 78-91.

24.Vladan, D. and N. Ljubica (2002)."Expert System in Finance-A Cross-Section of The Field».
www.citeseerx.ist.psu.edu/viewdoc/download?doi=10.1.1.12.3232&rep=rep1&type=pdf

25.Yang, D. and M. A. Vasarhelyi (2000). "The Application of Expert Systems In Accounting".www.scholar.google.com/scholar?q=The+Application+Of+Expert+Syst ems+In+Accounting+YANG+
and+Vasarhelyi&hl=fa&as_sdt=0&as_vis=1&oi=scholart.

26.Ying, H. S. (2007). "Understanding the impact of expert systems on auditors, information processingand decision outcomes". Afaanz Conference.

27.Abu-Musa, Ahmad A.(2002), "Computer Crimes: How Can YouProtect Your Computerized Accounting Information Systems", The Journal of American Academy of Business, Cambridge, USA, Vol. 2. No.1 September 2002, pp. 91-111 .

28. Davis, C. E.(1997)," An Assessment of Accounting Information Security", CPA Journal, March,:28·35

29. Qureshi, Anique A and Joel G Siegel(1997), "The accountant and computer security", The National Public Accountant; Washington, May .

30. Williams, Paul(1995), "Safe, Secure and up to Standard", Journal of Accountancy,(Apr. 1990) p. 60.

31.Charles e. davis. » an assessment of accounting information security«. The cpa journals. Vol 67.

32.Riner , Kelly Rex, Charles A. Snyder and Houston H. carr (1991). »risk analysis for information technology« management information system. vol 8

33.Melissa walters (2007). »a draft of an information systems security and control course«. Journals of information system. 5-34.

34.Wang Ry, StrondD (1996). Beyond accuracy »what data quality means to data costomers« . journal management information system.

35.Deborah BeardandH. Josephwen (2007). » Reducing the thereate level for

36.Daily C. and lueblfing, M. (2000)» . Defending the security of the accounting system«. The CPA Journals. 62-65.

37.Blakley B, E. Mcdermott and D. Geer. » information security in information risk manamement, in proceeding of NSPW«. Cloudcroft ,newmexico. USA, 2002

38.Ge. W. andS. Mcvay. 2005. »the disclosure of material weeknessein internal control after the Sarbanes «. oxleyact. Accounting Horizons 19 (3): 137- 158

39.Mihalache D. Avsenie- samoil. (2011). » security of the Accounting information system infrastructure«. 1339-1345

40.Ilhan. D, and veysi. n. t. 2001. Review of social , Economic &Bussiness studies

41.locity , M. C. and L. P Willcocks (1998). » an empirical investigation of information technology sourcing «. lessons from experience MIS Quarterly 22 (3). 363-408

42.Ling-yu, chou, Charles. Du, timon , S. Vincent, lai, (2007). » continuous auditing whit amulti agent system«. Decision support systems, No. 42. pp. 2274-2292.

www.ingramcontent.com/pod-product-compliance
Lightning Source LLC
La Vergne TN
LVHW042347060326
832902LV00006B/446